This book is dedicated to:

Tia and Grey Kitty for inspiring the character of Striped Kitty and to Kelly for letting me borrow your striped kitty for adventuring.

Special thanks to:

Shelb for the amazing illustrations, Liv for being my biggest cheerleader and a great editor, Isaac for inspiring this story, Peyton for always running ahead and to James for always adventuring with me in life & the great outdoors.

Land acknowledgment

We would like to start by acknowledging that the Maliseet Trail is situated on the traditional unceded territory of the Wolastoqiyik (Maliseet), Mi'kmaq and Peskotomuhkati peoples.

For more information on Dunroamin' Stray & Rescue:

Striped Kitty was sad.

It was adoption day at Dunroamin' and he did not think he would get adopted.
He was different from the other rescue cats.

All of a sudden the GoDo family burst in. They noticed Striped Kitty right away.

He WAS different and they knew he would fit right in. They could not wait to take him home!

When Striped Kitty arrived at their home, he realized his new family was different too.

The GoDo family was a wonderful family of all shapes and sizes.

Striped Kitty looked around and there were things EVERYWHERE!

But the family did not seem to notice the mess.

Everyone was as busy as bees!

They were up, they were down, they were all around!

In no time, Striped Kitty was a big part of the GoDo family. He felt so happy and loved!

"This is a great day!"
he thought.

After a few days, Striped Kitty realized the family loved going outside as much as he did. They liked going on something they called "hikes".

Mom told him they were going on a hiking adventure the very next day. Striped Kitty was very excited!

When Striped Kitty woke up, he thought to himself, "today is the day!"

Mom had a box for Striped Kitty.

When he opened the box, there were red shiny booties inside. They were just the right size!

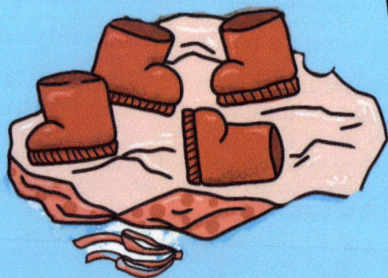

Mom said the booties would keep his paws warm and dry. He could not wait to try them.

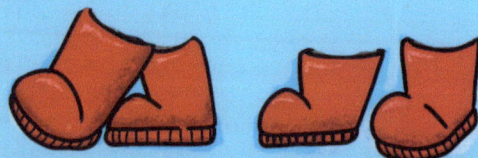

They packed up, piled everyone in, and set off on their hiking adventure. "Whatever that is", thought Striped Kitty.

After a short drive, they stopped by the side of the road.

Striped Kitty saw a sign that read:

MALISEET TRAIL

The family was bouncing when they got out of the van.

Everyone was so full of energy!

The air was cold, but the sun was bright. It felt warmer than it was. There was a bit of snow and the path was a little muddy.

The kids had been to this trail before, so they ran ahead knowing exactly where to go.

THEY WERE UP, THEY WERE DOWN,
THEY WERE ALL AROUND!

Striped Kitty wondered,

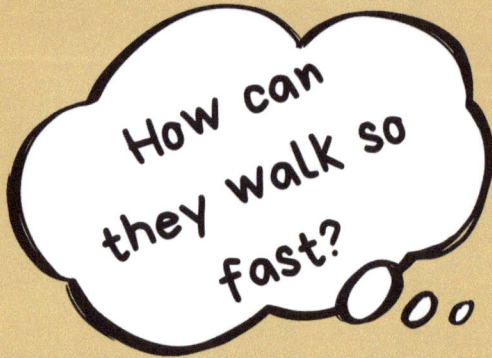

How can they walk so fast?

He saw the long climb in front of them
and thought to himself...

Striped Kitty was falling behind and he started to feel sad and angry.

He kept trying to lift his legs, but they did not want to move.

Each step was harder than the last.

"Why is this so hard?" he thought.

He tried every way he could.

He was not sure he liked hiking.

Then Mom turned and noticed Striped Kitty was falling behind. She smiled softly and waited.

She asked if he was tired. He said no.

She asked if he was cold. He said no.

She asked if he was hungry. He said no.

She asked him why he was upset. He told her he could not move his legs. The more he tried, the harder it got.
He needed help.

OHHH !! exclaimed Mom.

She knew exactly what to do.

She scooped up Striped Kitty and told him everything would be ok.

She pulled off his little red shiny hiking booties and put him down.

WOW he purred.

That felt so much better!

He skipped ahead of everyone! He smiled and thought...

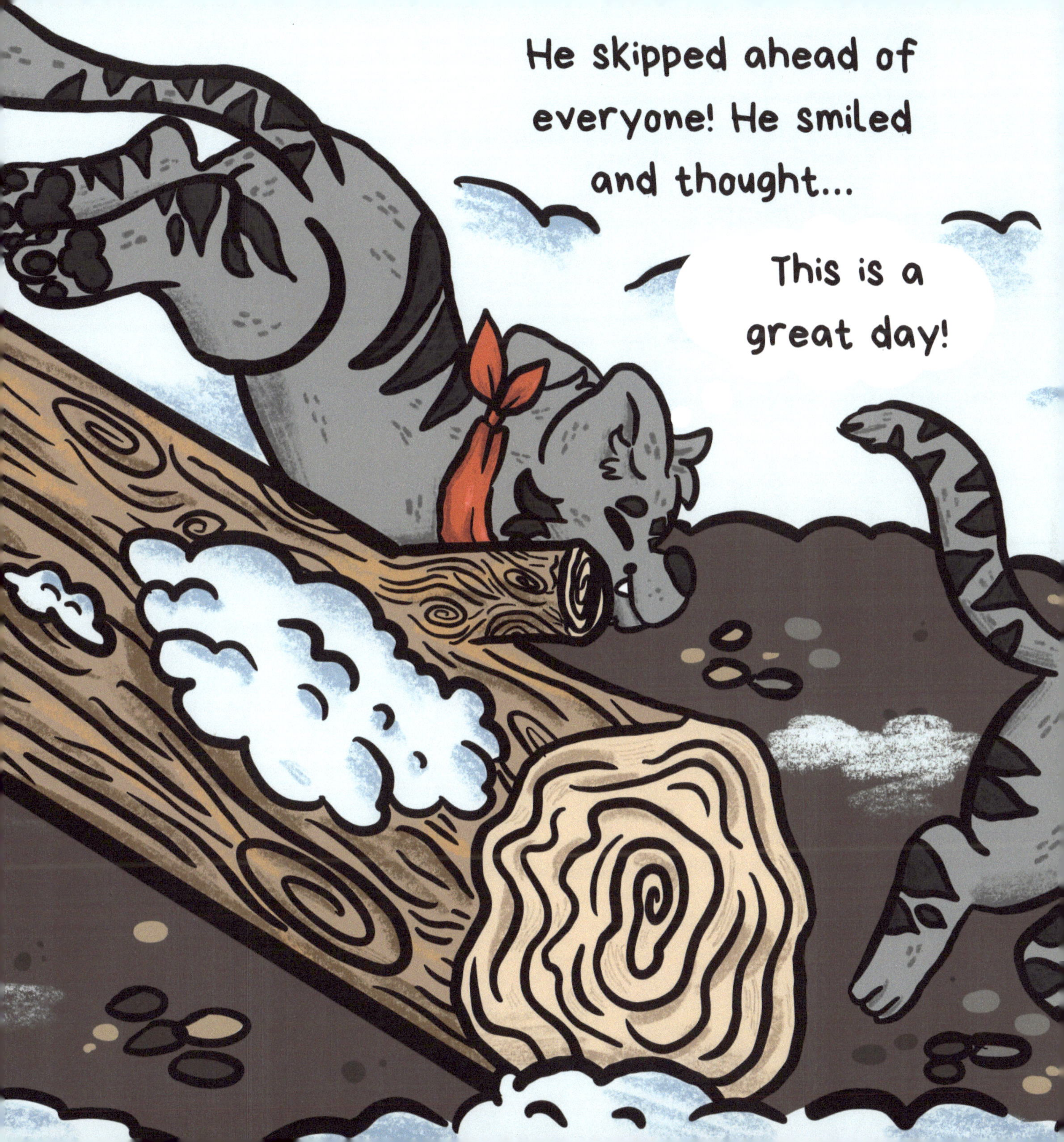

He looked all around and saw snow on the trees starting to drip.

As the sun shone on the snow, it sparkled like diamonds.

The trail led down a steep path. Down, down, down they went.

Just then, Striped Kitty heard a SCARY sound.

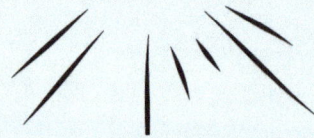

His tail became big and fluffy.

Was it a jet plane? Was it a vacuum cleaner? Where was the sound coming from?

It was a beautiful WATERFALL!!
It was so lovely, so peaceful, and so....
LOUD!!
WHOOSH
The water flowed as fast as a rollercoaster!

Everyone yelled really loudly but they could not hear each other.
They sang. They danced.
They were up, they were down, they were all around !
Striped Kitty was having the time of his life !

After a snack, they packed up and started back.

Up, up, up they climbed.

Striped Kitty was thinking as he hiked. He started the day thinking he could not do this.

He struggled but he kept going and going. He did it, with a little help.

He learned that sometimes things start off badly, but they end up getting better. It is always a good idea to try.

He was **UP** he was **DOWN**

and **Love** was all around.

You never know what might happen when you try your best.

he thought.

He also learned to ask for help when he needs it.

In the end, Striped Kitty had an amazing day.

Striped Kitty became an ADVENTURE CAT!

He loved hiking with his new family, and he was excited for the many adventures to come.

Today was a great day !

The End

Striped Kitty's
Hiking Adventure Checklist
(for kids and parents)

Pack:

- a water bottle
- snacks
- small first aid kit
- compass
- hat
- rain gear
- sunscreen
- bug spray
- cell phone or satellite device

Wear:

- layers
- appropriate footwear

Do:

- let others know when and where you are going.
- your homework on trails before you leave.

www.ingramcontent.com/pod-product-compliance
Lightning Source LLC
Chambersburg PA
CBHW042014080426
42734CB00003B/71